Minibeasts

Calling all aliens!

Are you planning a holiday to planet Earth?

'Minibeasts'

Published by MAVERICK ARTS PUBLISHING LTD

Studio 11, City Business Centre, 6 Brighton Road,

Horsham, West Sussex, RH13 5BB, +44 (0)1403 256941

© Maverick Arts Publishing Limited November 2019

A CIP catalogue record for this book is available at the British Library.

ISBN 978-1-84886-634-8

www.maverickbooks.co.uk

Credits:

Finn & Zeek illustrations by Jake McDonald, Bright Illustration Agency

Cover: Jake McDonald/Bright, Staffan Widstrand/Wild Wonders of China/Naturepl.com
Inside: **Naturepl.com:** Alex Hyde (6, 8, 16), MYN/Dirk Funhoff (9), Paul Harcourt
Davies (10), Nick Upton (11), Stephen Dalton (11, 13), Terry Whittaker/2020VISION
(12), Philip Dalton (13), Edwin Giesbers (14), Ingo Arndt (14, 21), Konrad
Wothe/Minden (14), Kim Taylor (16), MYN/Paul van Hoof (16), Chris Mattison (17),
Wild Wonders of Europe/Benvie (17), Thomas Marent/Minden (18, 22), Daniel Heuclin
(18), Magnus Lundgren/Wild Wonders of China (19), Pete Oxford/Minden (19, 23),
Pedro Narra (19), Mark Bowler (19), Matthew Maran (19), Phil Savoie (20), Piotr
Naskrecki/Minden (21), David Welling (21), Phil Savoie (24), Staffan Widstrand/Wild
Wonders of China (27).

Orange

This book is rated as: Orange Band (Guided Reading)
This story is decodable at Letters and Sounds Phase 5.

Minibeasts

Contents

INCOMING MESSAGE

Dear Finn and Zeek,

We have just got back from a trip to Earth. We saw lots and lots of minibeasts! But why do they all look so different?

Please explain!

From,
Beet and Lil
(Planet Juice)

Minibeasts are small animals without a backbone. They are also known as **invertebrates**. Spiders, snails, beetles, worms and caterpillars are all minibeasts.

Come on, Finn! Let's go see some minibeasts.

Minibeasts look different for many reasons.

Bush cricket

Bodies

Some minibeasts have body parts like this:

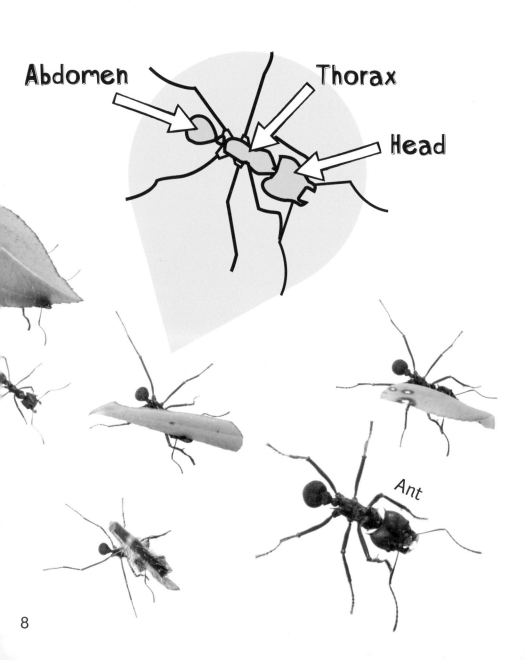

Abdomen

Thorax

Head

Ant

Other minibeasts, like worms, have one main body part. It is split into sections.

Earthworm

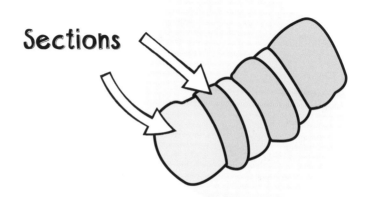

Sections

Wings

Some minibeasts have wings.

This moth has **opaque** wings.

Crimson-speckled moth

This dragonfly has **transparent** wings. They look weak, but really they are strong!

Darter dragonfly

Beetles have two sets of wings. One set is hard, like a cover. The other set is used for flying.

Cover

Ladybird

Flying

Exoskeletons

Some minibeasts have exoskeletons. This is a hard cover that protects a minibeast's body.

Exoskeleton

Stag beetle

Exoskeleton

Exoskeletons are made from something called **chitin**. Ants, spiders and beetles all have exoskeletons.

This little guy has just shed his old exoskeleton!

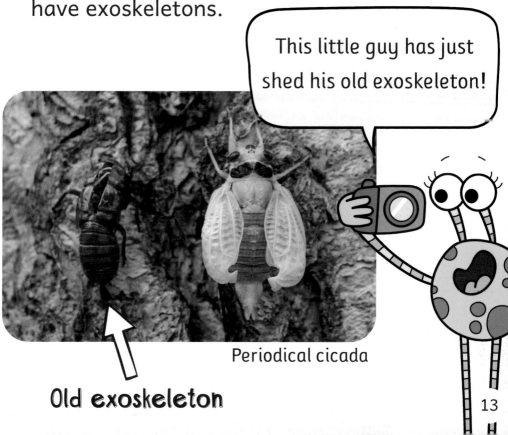

Periodical cicada

Old exoskeleton

13

Shells

Shells are a type of exoskeleton.

They are very tough and help minibeasts

to stay safe from **predators**.

Burgundy snail

Land snail

When snails grow bigger, their shells grow with them.

Legs

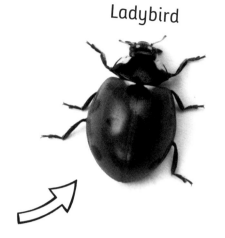

Minibeasts can have
a different number
of legs. Insects are
minibeasts with 6 legs.

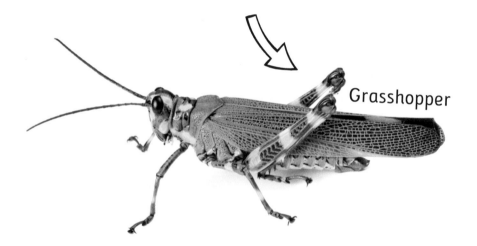

Grasshopper

Other minibeasts have no legs,
like slugs and worms.

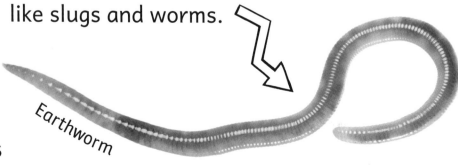

Earthworm

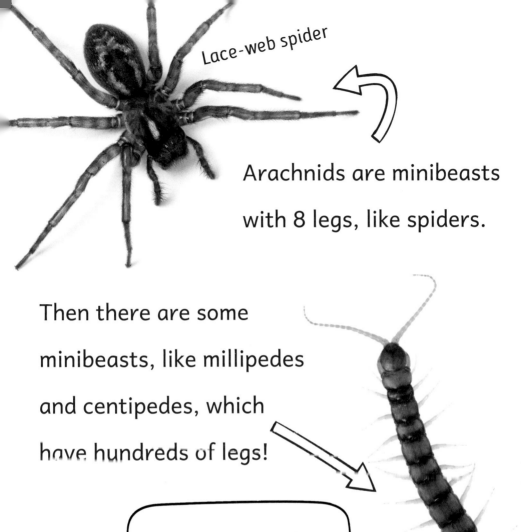

Lace-web spider

Arachnids are minibeasts with 8 legs, like spiders.

Then there are some minibeasts, like millipedes and centipedes, which have hundreds of legs!

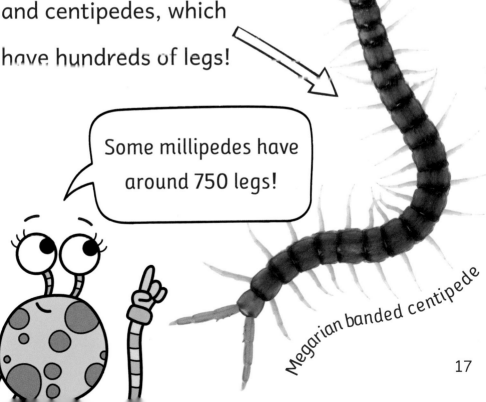

Some millipedes have around 750 legs!

Megarian banded centipede

17

Colours

Minibeasts use colours as **camouflage.** Camouflage helps minibeasts hide because they blend in with what's around them.

Orchid mantis

Stick grasshopper

That one looks like a flower!

And that one looks like a stick.

Lantern bug

Some minibeasts use bright colours to keep predators away. The bright colours say, "I'm dangerous! Don't eat me!"

Some minibeasts look like other animals to confuse predators.

Owl butterfly

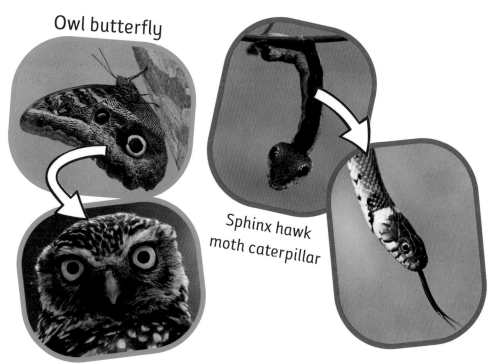

Sphinx hawk moth caterpillar

Texture

Some minibeasts are furry so that **pollen** will stick to their legs.

Honeybee

Others are spiky to stop animals eating them!

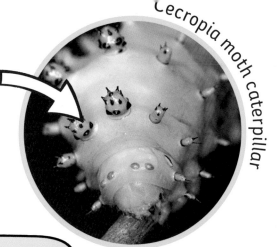
Cecropia moth caterpillar

Predator bugs also use spikes to catch their **prey**!

Katydid

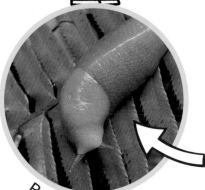
Banana slug

Other minibeasts are slimy and sticky to help them glide and climb.

Antennae

Antennae are like extra-long noses for minibeasts! They help minibeasts to smell and taste things.

Forest cockchafer beetle

Look at that guy!

Tongues

Some minibeasts have long tongues.

They use them like straws to get **nectar**.

Orange tiger butterfly

Butterflies taste through their feet! How weird is that!?

Senses

Most minibeasts don't have good hearing or sight, so they have better senses of taste, touch and smell.

This is why flowers are bright and smell nice. It is to attract minibeasts!

MESSAGE SENT

Dear Beet and Lil,

As you said, minibeasts look very different! Their amazing features help them to find food and stay safe.

Next time you're on Earth, be sure to see the rhinoceros beetle - it's our favourite!

From,
Finn and Zeek x

Rhinoceros beetle

1. What are invertebrates?
a) Big animals with a backbone
b) Small animals without a backbone
c) Small animals with a backbone

2. What are the parts of a worm's body called?
a) Sections
b) Chunks
c) Rolls

3. What is a six-legged minibeast called?
a) An arachnid
b) An insect
c) A worm

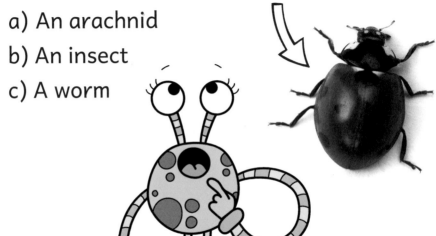

4. Why might a minibeast have bright colours?
a) To catch predators
b) To look pretty
c) To scare away predators

5. How does pollen stick to minibeasts?
a) It sticks to their furry legs
b) They use slime to catch it
c) They use spikes

6. Why do some minibeasts have long tongues?
a) To scare away predators
b) To attract other minibeasts
c) To get nectar from flowers

Turn over for answers

Index/Glossary

Camouflage pg 18
A way of hiding by blending into the surroundings.

Chitin pg 13
A tough substance in minibeasts' exoskeletons.

Invertebrate pg 6
A creature without a backbone.

Nectar pg 23
A sugary liquid made by plants.

Opaque pg 10
Something that you cannot see through, like a piece of cardboard or a wall.

Pollen pg 20

A substance used by plants to make seeds.

Predator pg 14, 19, 21

A creature that hunts other creatures (prey).

Prey pg 21

A creature that is hunted by another creature (predator).

Transparent pg 11

Something clear that you can see through, like glass.

Book Bands for Guided Reading

The Institute of Education book banding system is a scale of colours that reflects the various levels of reading difficulty. The bands are assigned by taking into account the content, the language style, the layout and phonics. Word, phrase and sentence level work is also taken into consideration.

Maverick Early Readers are a bright, attractive range of books covering the pink to white bands. All of these books have been book banded for guided reading to the industry standard and edited by a leading educational consultant.

Fiction

Non-fiction

To view the whole Maverick Readers scheme, visit our website at www.maverickearlyreaders.com

Or scan the QR code above to view our scheme instantly!

Pink
Red
Yellow
Blue
Green
Orange
Turquoise
Purple
Gold
White